PRODUCTS: FROM IDEA TO MARKET

Candy

FOCUS READERS®
BEACON

by Abby Doty

www.focusreaders.com

Copyright © 2025 by Focus Readers®, Mendota Heights, MN 55120. All rights reserved. No part of this book may be reproduced or utilized in any form or by any means without written permission from the publisher.

Focus Readers is distributed by North Star Editions:
sales@northstareditions.com | 888-417-0195

Produced for Focus Readers by Red Line Editorial.

Photographs ©: iStockphoto, cover, 1, 8, 12, 25, 26, 29; Shutterstock Images, 4, 6, 11, 14, 17, 18, 21, 22

Library of Congress Cataloging-in-Publication Data
Library of Congress Cataloging-in-Publication Data is available on the Library of Congress website.

ISBN
979-8-88998-404-7 (hardcover)
979-8-88998-432-0 (paperback)
979-8-88998-485-6 (ebook pdf)
979-8-88998-460-3 (hosted ebook)

Printed in the United States of America
Mankato, MN
012025

About the Author

Abby Doty is a writer, editor, and booklover from Minnesota.

Table of Contents

CHAPTER 1

All Kinds of Candy 5

CHAPTER 2

New Ideas 9

CHAPTER 3

Making Candy 15

THAT'S AMAZING!

Candy for Everyone 20

CHAPTER 4

From Company to Customer 23

Focus Questions • 28

Glossary • 30

To Learn More • 31

Index • 32

CHAPTER 1

All Kinds of Candy

A boy and his mother walk through a candy store. Each shelf holds many kinds of candy. The packages shine with bright colors. They all look tasty.

 Candy sales make billions of dollars in the United States each year.

Some rock candy comes in tiny pieces. Other times, it comes on sticks.

The mom and boy make their choice. They buy a small bag of rock candy. It includes many flavors. Some pieces taste like watermelon. Others taste like grape, strawberry, or orange. When the boy gets home, he tries some. The rock candy pops and fizzes in his mouth. It makes a crackling noise, too.

The boy has never had candy like this before. He wonders how someone came up with the idea. And he wonders how people made it.

Did You Know?

People have been making candy for thousands of years.

CHAPTER 2

New Ideas

Candy companies make new candy all the time. First, company workers **brainstorm** different ideas. They may ask **customers** for thoughts. Often, businesses make flavors that are already popular.

Companies may create new flavors of existing candy.

9

For example, many companies make fruit candy. Other companies might choose to do the same.

Candy companies also choose a **target audience**. Some customers want healthy candy. Others like bright, sugary candy. Businesses keep those audiences in mind.

After picking new ideas, companies begin creating their candy. Many companies make candy in **laboratories**. Workers try out different recipes. Some

Food scientists test out their ideas in laboratories.

recipes are sweeter. Some make the candy thicker. Companies work on the candy's look, too. The color and shape can tell customers the flavor. For example, lemon-flavored candy may be yellow. Pieces may be shaped like lemons.

A tester may share opinions about a candy's size and feel.

After creation, new candy still needs more testing. Focus groups often help companies. People in these groups try candy that isn't in stores yet. They give their thoughts on its taste and look. Companies use those opinions. They might make changes to their candy.

Companies may spend months or years creating new candies. The design and taste must be just right. When a **product** is finally perfect, companies are ready. They decide to make more and sell the candy.

Did You Know?

Since 1928, more than 60 new candy products have been part of the Reese's brand.

CHAPTER 3

Making Candy

Making candy takes many steps. First, a business needs **ingredients**. Different types of candy use different ingredients. Chocolate candy usually needs milk and sugar. It uses cocoa, too.

Many popular candies include caramel or nuts.

Hard candy requires sugar, food coloring, and flavoring. Companies get these ingredients from farms, stores, and food scientists. Some ingredients are cheap and easy to get. Others may be expensive or come from far away.

Next, it is time to make lots of the candy. Large companies use factories. Machines create the candy. One machine weighs each ingredient. Another machine mixes the ingredients together.

Factory workers check the candy that machines make. They make sure everything looks right.

And another shapes the candy using a mold. Each piece of candy looks nearly the same.

Smaller companies may make candy by hand. They can do this in their stores or at home. This process can take a long time.

17

Small companies may have kitchens in the backs of their stores.

And each piece may be a little different. But making candy by hand can be cheaper for small companies. Large machines cost a lot of money.

Next, machines or people package the candy. Small companies often

18

sell the wrapped candy from their own stores. Large companies usually need trucks to move the products. Trucks transport candy to **retailers**. These places include candy stores, grocery stores, and gas stations. In stores, customers can finally buy the candy.

Did You Know?
Some factories make millions of candies each day.

THAT'S AMAZING!

Candy for Everyone

Chocolate usually includes animal products. For example, it often uses dairy. Most companies make milk chocolate with cow's milk. Some chocolate may have cream or eggs, too. However, many people cannot eat these foods.

In the 2020s, some big candy companies addressed this problem. They created new chocolate products. The new products didn't use dairy. Some didn't include other animal products, either. Instead, they used ingredients such as oat milk. That way, more people could eat this chocolate.

▶ **Dark chocolate does not use milk. White chocolate has no cocoa.**

CHAPTER 4

From Company to Customer

Retailers sell many kinds of candy. Companies hope customers choose their products instead of others. A candy's packaging can help. Wrappers often use bright colors. Those colors stand out.

Candy wrappers often show the candy's name in large writing.

Companies can also use popular trends. For example, some colors are more popular each year than others. More people may buy candy that uses trendy colors.

Companies also **advertise** their candy. Many businesses use **commercials**. Billboards and websites are also common. Some customers care about eating healthy foods. So, ads point out how healthy the candy is. Other customers care about the planet.

▶ **Ads might show off a candy's new sizes or flavors.**

These customers may want candy with recyclable packaging. Ads can tell people those details.

Companies also try to point out their candy's special features. For example, many chocolate candies melt when people pick them up.

Customers buy more candy canes in December.

A business could show that their chocolate doesn't melt. Maybe a candy has a flavor no other company used before. Ads can point out the candy's unique flavor.

Other candies may be seasonal. Customers can only buy them

during certain seasons or holidays. So, companies use the time limit to advertise. They tell customers to buy it before it's gone.

In the end, customers make their candy choices. If the process goes well, customers and companies are both happy.

Did You Know?

Colors can help people feel certain emotions. For example, a red wrapper can make customers feel hungrier.

Focus Questions

Write your answers on a separate piece of paper.

1. Write a few sentences explaining how people create ideas for new candy.

2. If you could create a new candy, what would it taste like?

3. What is the first step of making candy after the ideas are ready?
   - **A.** packaging the candy
   - **B.** putting candy into molds
   - **C.** getting the ingredients

4. Why might big companies need trucks to move their products?
   - **A.** They sell candy in only one store.
   - **B.** They sell huge amounts of candy.
   - **C.** They sell candy close to the factory.

5. What does **requires** mean in this book?

*Chocolate candy usually needs milk and sugar. It uses cocoa, too. Hard candy **requires** sugar, food coloring, and flavoring.*

    A. must have
    B. looks like
    C. creates a lot of

6. What does **unique** mean in this book?

*Maybe a candy has a flavor no other company used before. Ads can point out the candy's **unique** flavor.*

    A. small
    B. different
    C. old

Answer key on page 32.

29

Glossary

advertise

To make messages or videos about a product so customers want to buy it.

brainstorm

To make new ideas by considering all possibilities and letting thoughts flow freely.

commercials

Messages or videos to sell a product. They appear during other programs.

customers

People who buy products.

ingredients

Foods that are mixed together to make a different food.

laboratories

Places with equipment to practice science and test products.

product

An item that is for sale.

retailers

Businesses that sell products to customers.

target audience

A group of customers that a company wants to sell to.

To Learn More

BOOKS

Grack, Rachel. *Cocoa Bean to Chocolate.*
Minneapolis: Bellwether Media, 2020.

Hill, Christina. *Supply Chains in Infographics.* Ann
Arbor, MI: Cherry Lake Press, 2023.

Koster, Gloria. *The Story of Chocolate.* North
Mankato, MN: Capstone Press, 2024.

NOTE TO EDUCATORS

Visit **www.focusreaders.com** to find lesson plans,
activities, links, and other resources related to
this title.

Index

A
advertising, 24–27
animal products, 20

B
brainstorming, 9

C
chocolate, 15, 20, 25–26
commercials, 24
customers, 9–11, 19, 23–27

D
dairy, 20

F
flavors, 6, 9, 11, 16, 26
focus groups, 12
food scientists, 16

H
health, 10, 24

I
ingredients, 15–16, 20

L
laboratories, 10

M
machines, 16, 18

P
packaging, 5, 18, 23, 25
product, 13, 19, 20, 23

R
retailers, 19, 23
rock candy, 6–7

S
sugar, 10, 15–16

W
wrappers, 19, 23, 27